# Crochet For

# Beginners

**2<sup>nd</sup> Edition**

Learn to Crochet Quickly & Easily

Along With 15 Step-By-Step Patterns

by Kitty Moore

# Table of Contents

# Introduction

Crochet is easy to learn and requires very little investment. You can accomplish a crochet project the first day you pick up a crochet hook! There are many other reasons why crochet has become such a popular phenomenon.

- It's relaxing! You can crochet while you have a conversation, or while you watch television.

- It's portable! You can stick a crochet project in your pocket and take it wherever you go. Whenever you're waiting in a doctor's office, at a school, or anywhere, you always have a project to keep yourself busy!
- It's expressive! You can utilize a variety of materials, colors, and stitches.

- It's personal! You can create gifts that are unique and individual.

- It's versatile! You can crochet with thin thread to make lace doilies or with a bulky yarn to make a warm hat or vest.

## But wait, there is more!

- Crochet has a long history. Crocheted items were found in ancient China and along Arab trade routes.

- Crochet is also a contemporary art form. "Yarn bombers" around the world have crocheted cars, bicycles, fire hydrants, and signposts in cities and industrial areas.

- Crochet is scientific. Hyperbolic Crochet is the combination of crochet and mathematics. It is used to create models of the disappearing corals of the Great Barrier Reef around Australia, and to crochet replacement reefs from recycled trash.

Crochet is a dynamic skill! Learning to crochet can be a practical, useful activity. It might even begin a lifetime fascination with fashion, art, or mathematics.

# Crochet Supplies

Learning to crochet requires very little initial investment. Start with the basic materials, and practice the beginning stitches. After you have mastered the fundamentals, you can investigate the huge variety of hooks, yarns and patterns that are available.

## Crochet Hooks

- Crochet hooks come in a number of sizes and materials, but start simple.

- Use only one hook as you learn your first stitches and complete your first project.

- Start with an aluminium hook in size J.

## Yarn

- Yarn also comes in a wide variety of weights and textures. Again, start simple.

- Use an inexpensive yarn.

- Choose a smooth, light-coloured yarn that will allow you to easily see your stitches.

- Select a heavy yarn—labelled "worsted" or "chunky." It will be easier to handle.

# Scissors

- A small, sharp pair of sewing scissors will be perfect.

# Must Knows

## Crochet Hooks

The size of the crochet hook determines the size of your stitches. A crochet pattern will call for a specific-sized hook, but sometimes the right sized hook is hard to find. That is because crochet hooks come in different sizes based on the material, brand and country where they were produced. A conversion tables can help you find the hook you need.

## Crochet Hook Material

- Aluminium hooks are smooth and easy to use. They and available in a wide variety of sizes.

- Plastic hooks are light weight and also come in jumbo size.

- Bamboo hooks are available in many sizes and are light and warm.

- Steel hooks are usually small hooks used to crochet fine thread.

## Crochet Yarn

Many fibers can be crocheted. Fibers are evaluated for seven qualities: absorbency, breathability, dye ability, softness, loft, resiliency and thickness. A pattern will usually suggest a specific yarn for a project. There are three categories of yarn fibers: plant fibers, animal fibers and synthetic fibers.

# Terms

Crochet has its own vocabulary that you will encounter when you read a crochet pattern. Here are some of the most frequently used terms and abbreviations.

- **Chain stitch**, **ch.** Basic crochet stitch. These interlocking yarn circles form your first line of crochet. See *how to chain stitch* directions below.

- **Decrease, dec.** Eliminate one or more stitches.

- **Double Crochet, dc.** One of the basic crochet stitches. See *how to double crochet* directions below.

- **Half Double Crochet, hdc.** One of the basic crochet stitches. See *how to half double crochet* directions below.

- **Increase, inc.** Add one or more stitches.

- **Join.** Join two stitches together, usually using a slip stitch.

- **Single Crochet stitch**, **sc.** Basic crochet stitch. This stitch will connect to the chain stitch. You can make your first project using just the chain and single crochet stitch. See *how to single crochet* directions below.

- **Skein.** The yarn you buy comes in a coiled arrangement called a skein. Working from the skein cause tangles. To make your crocheting life simpler, take the time to wrap the yarn into a large ball.

- **Repeat.** Do again.

- **Slip knot.** The beginning stitch in crochet. The initial yarn circle. See *how to make a slip knot* directions below.

- **Slip stitch, sl st.** Used to join the beginning and end of a line. See *how to slip stitch* directions below.

- **Triple crochet, tr or trc.** Basic crochet stitch. See *how to triple crochet* directions below.

- **Tunisian Crochet.** This combination of crochet and knitting uses a long crochet hook with a stopper at the end to keep the stitches from falling off the hook.

- **Turn.** Turn your work so you can work back for the next row.

# I have included a bonus just for you…

**FOR A LIMITED TIME ONLY** – Get my best-selling book "DIY Crafts: The 100 Most Popular Crafts & Projects That Make Your Life Easier" absolutely FREE!

Readers who have downloaded the bonus book as well have seen the greatest changes in their crafting abilities and have expanded their repertoire of crafts – so it is *highly recommended* to get this bonus book today!

# Get your free copy at:

# ArtsCraftsAndMore.com/Bonus

# Crochet Basics

## How to Make a Slip Knot

*These are right-handed instructions.*

1. Place the yarn between the index finger and thumb of your left hand. Weave the yarn loosely over your index finger, underneath your second and third fingers, and then up and over your pinkie finger. The tail of the yarn will fall below your left thumb.

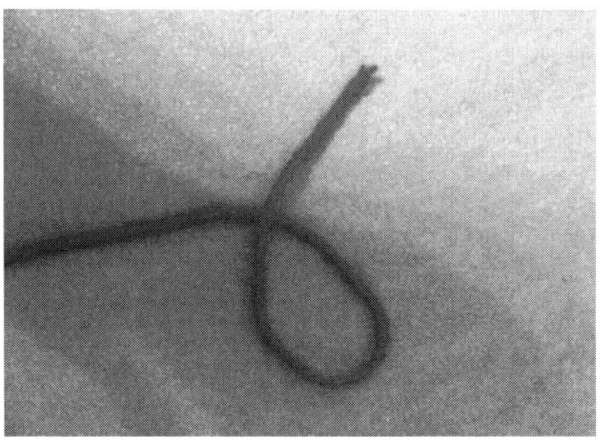

2. Hold the crochet hook gently in your right hand using the right thumb, index finger and middle finger. Place the crochet hook under the yarn on your left finger. Twist the yarn counter clockwise so that a loop of yarn is on the hook.

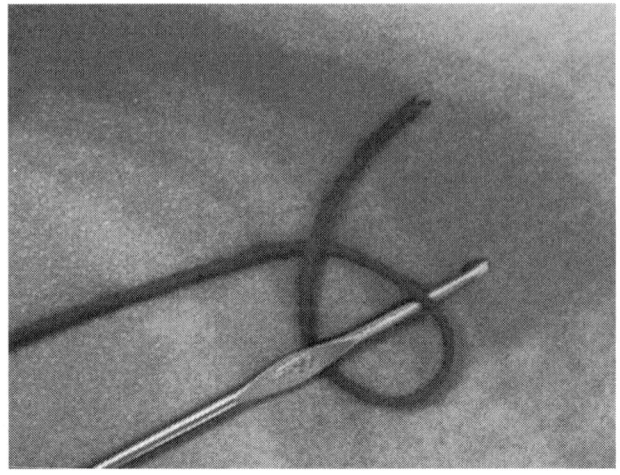

3.  Hold this yarn loop open with your left thumb. Hook the yarn dangling behind the loop and pull it through the loop from the back to the front.

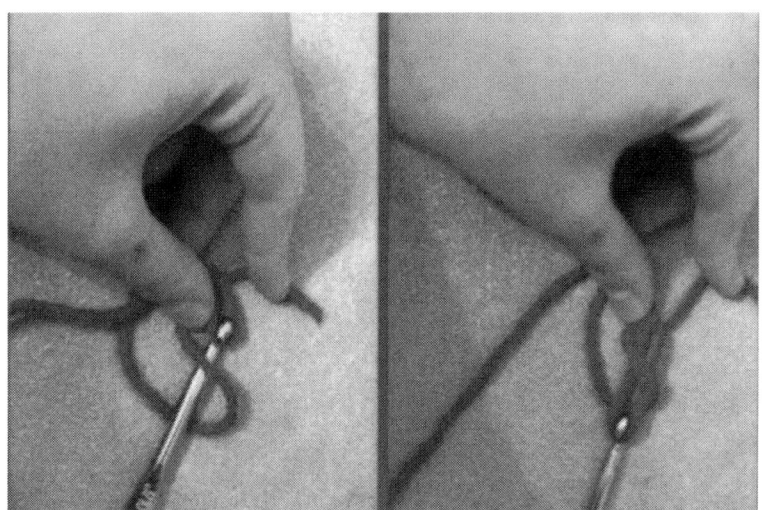

4.  Tighten both ends of the yarn. This is the slip knot. It will serve as the anchor to your crochet.

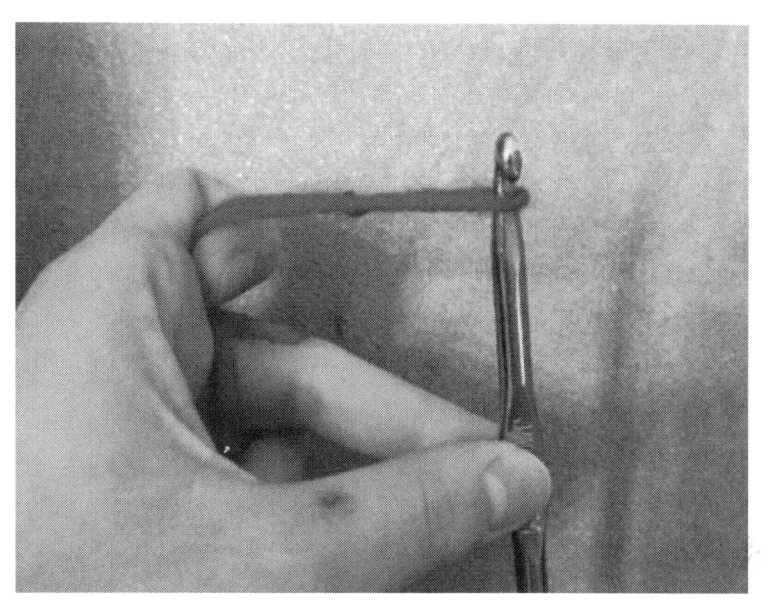

# How to Crochet a Chain Stitch

1. Hold the slip knot in your left hand facing you, with the crochet hook in the knot facing the palm of your left hand. With the crochet hook still in the knot, hook the length of yarn behind the knot and twist it counter clockwise. You have two loops on the crochet hook.

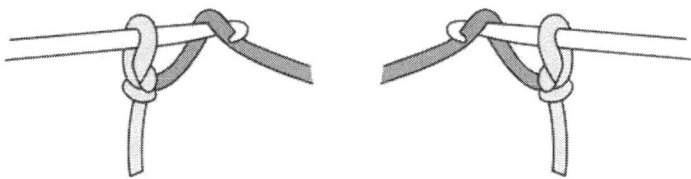

2. Now bring the yarn through the slip knot. This is your first chain. Repeat. Feed the yarn over your left forefinger. Hold the emerging chains between your left forefinger and thumb. The goal is to have the chains be the same size. To do this you must keep your hands relaxed. Maintain equal tension on each stitch with the weaving of the yarn over the left forefinger, under the second two fingers, and up and over the pinkie finger.

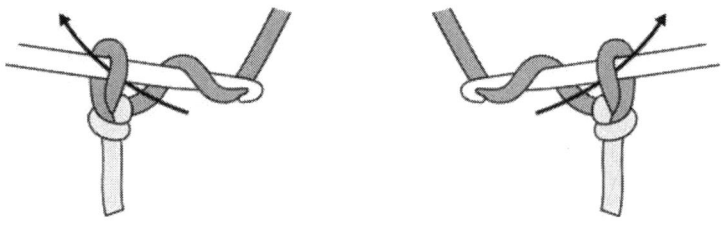

**Practice exercise:** Make a chain of 12 equal stitches. Unravel it. Make a chain of 20. Unravel it. Make a chain of 30. Unravel it. Now you are ready to move on!

# Single Crochet Stitch

1. Start with one slip knot and 8 chains. Turn the chain so that it faces away from you. Place the crochet hook in the front of the second chain, into the center of the V, and through the back of the chain. Now you have two loops on the crochet hook. Skip the first chain. You will usually do this unless the pattern states otherwise. Bring your yarn over the hook from the back to the front. Pull the yarn through both hoops. Now there is one chain on the hook. You have completed your first single crochet stitch!

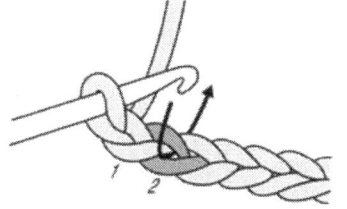 

2. Repeat. Place the crochet hook in front of the third chain, into the center of the V, and through the back of the chain. You will have two chains on the shaft of the crochet hook. Bring the yarn over the hook from the back to the front. Pull the yarn through the two loops. This is your second single crochet stitch. Continue until you have finished the row.

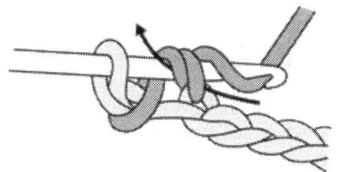 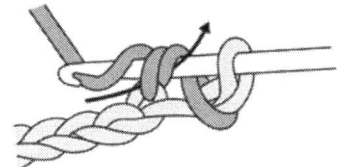

## Second Row

3. Turn the row of completed sc counter clockwise, keeping the hook in the last chain. Chain one stitch. This is called the turning stitch.

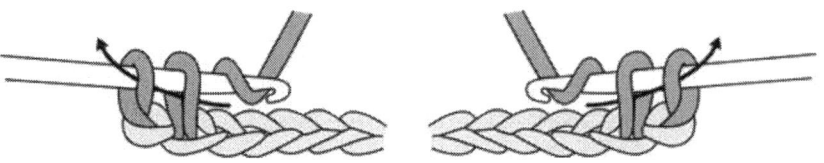

4. Skip the first stitch. Now single crochet in **the last stitch of the previous row**, not the center of the V. (You crochet in the center of the V only in the first row, the foundation row.) Continue to single crochet the rest of the row, turn the fabric counter clockwise, chain one, and repeat.

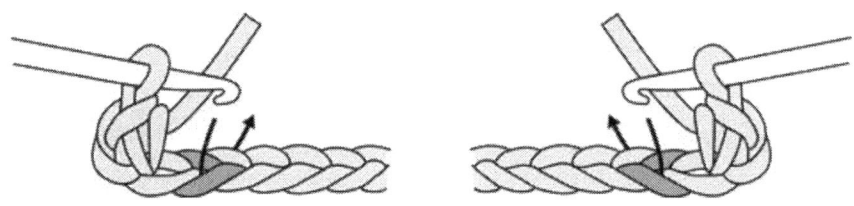

## Fastening Off

5. When the crochet is as long as you would like it, finish the last row and cut the yarn, leaving 6 inches. Draw the hook up through the stitch bringing the 6-inch tail of thread completely through. Pull it tightly to close.

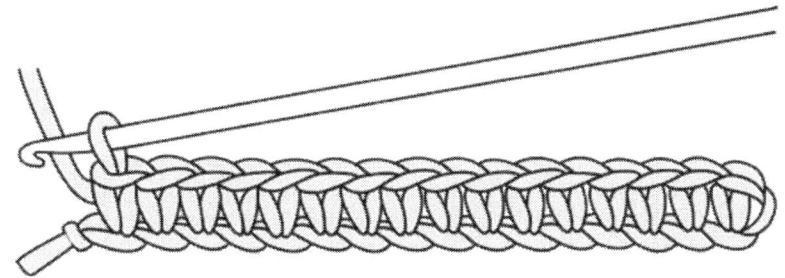

## Double Crochet Stitch

1. Make a slip knot. Chain 14 stitches. Turn the chain in your hand counter clockwise, keeping the hook in the last chain. Bring the yarn over the hook back to front, **skip the first three chains**, and then insert the hook in the front of the fourth chain. Draw the yarn through the chain stitch and onto the crochet hook. Now you will have three loops on the hook.

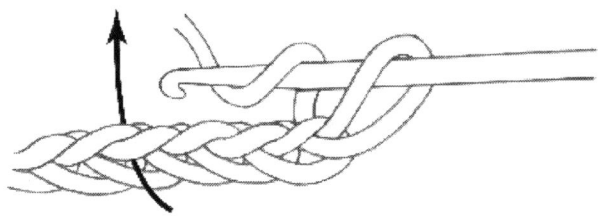

2. Yarn over the hook, back to the front. Draw yarn through first two loops on the hook. You now have two hoops on the hook. Yarn over the hook, back to the front. Draw through both loops. You now have one loop on the hook. You have completed the first double crochet! Continue the row. You will have 12 double crochets.

## Second Row

3. Turn counter clockwise. Chain 3. Skip the first double crochet. Bring the hook through the top of the second double crochet.

4. Work a double crochet into each of the remaining stitches. There should be 12 stitches. (The first three chains at the beginning of the row count as one dc.) Turn and repeat.

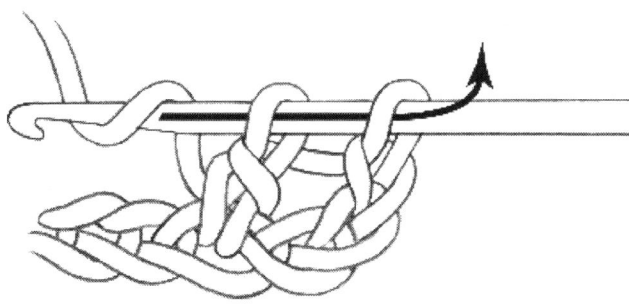

## Fastening Off

5. When the crochet fabric is as long as you would like, finish the last row and cut the yarn, leaving 6

inches. Draw the hook straight up through the stitch, bringing the 6-inch thread completely through. Pull it tightly to close.

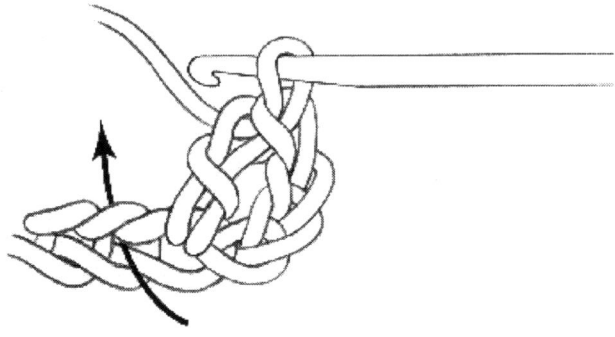

# Slip Stitch

## Slip Stitch to Join A Round

1.  When you have a foundation chain at the beginning of a project, you can form a round by connecting the two ends of the chain.  Insert the crochet hook into the first loop of the chain, yarn over.  There are now two chains on the crochet hook.

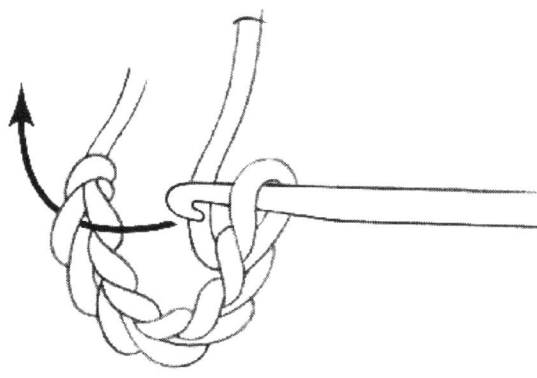

2.  Pull the yarn through both loops in one motion. The slip stitch holds the first and last chains together in a round.

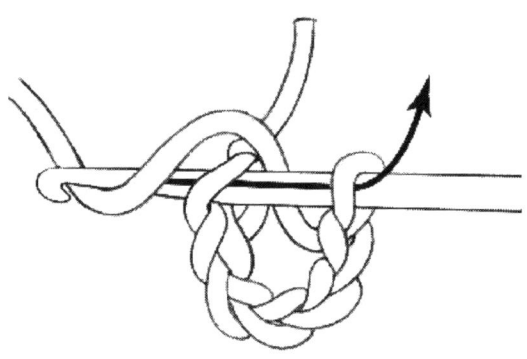

## Slip Stitch in a Row of Stitches

3. A slip stitch can also be used to join stitches or
   edges. Insert the crochet hook under two loops of
   the next stitch in a row of stitches. Yarn over. Draw
   the yarn through the loops of the stitch in one
   motion. This is a completed slip stitch.

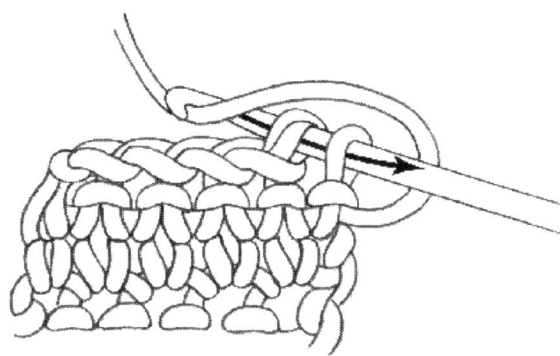

# Half Double Crochet Stitch

1. Make a slip knot.  Chain 12 stitches. Chain two more stitches.  Yarn over.

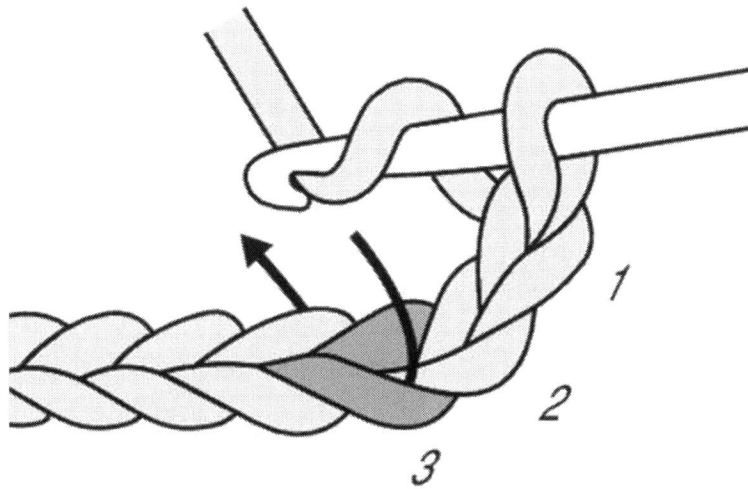

2. Insert crochet hook into the third chain from the hook. Pull the yarn through the center of the stitch. Yarn over. Draw the yarn through all three loops on the hook.

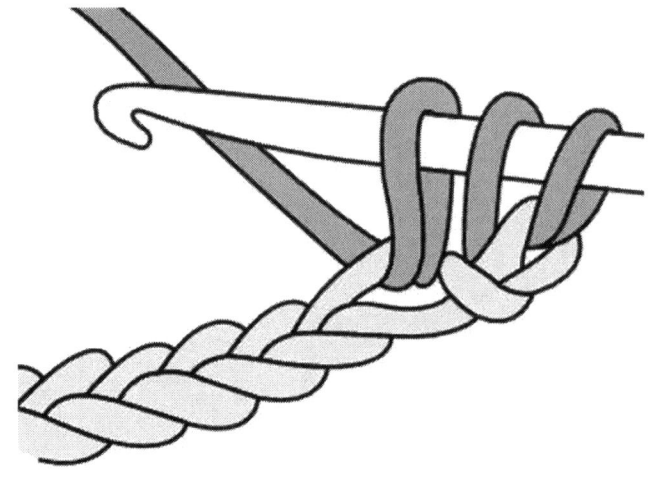

3. Insert the crochet hook into the next chain. This is a half double stitch. Continue the rest of the row. You will have 12 half double stitches including the initial chain stitch at the front of the row.

**Second Row**

4. Turn counter clockwise. Chain two. Yarn over. Skip one stitch. Insert hook in second half double stitch.

Complete row. You should have 12 half double stitches.

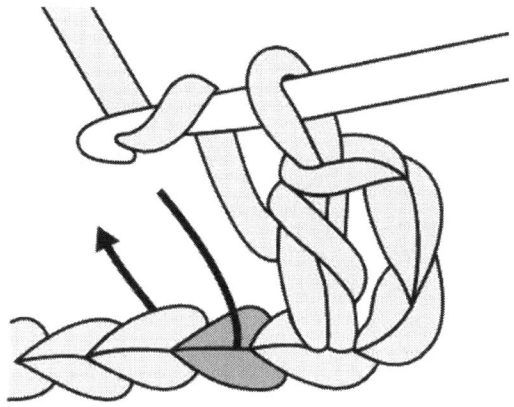

**Fastening Off**

5. When the crochet is as long as you would like, finish the last row and cut the yarn, leaving 6 inches. Draw the hook strait up through the stitch bringing the 6-inch thread completely through.  Pull it tightly to close.

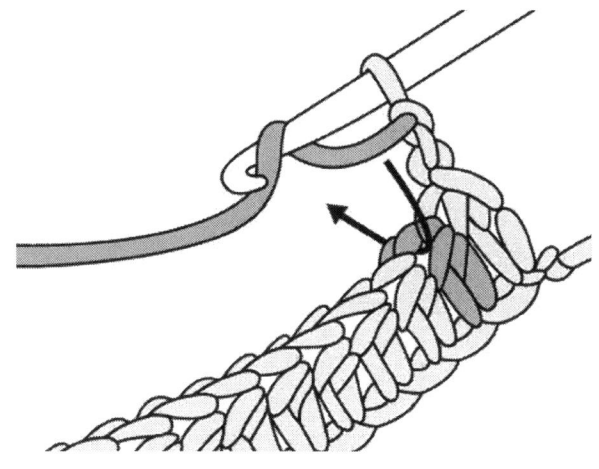

# Treble Crochet, or Triple Crochet

1.  Start with one slip knot and 12 chains. Turn. Yarn over twice. You will have four loops on the hook.

2.  Yarn over. Draw the yarn through two loops. Yarn over. Draw yarn through two loops.

3.  Yarn over again, and draw the yarn through two loops. This is your triple crochet stitch. Repeat on the remaining chains. You will have 12 stitches.

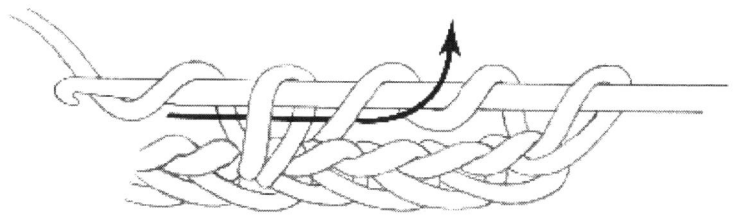

## Second Row

4. Turn counter clockwise. Chain 4. Insert hook into the second triple crochet stitch.

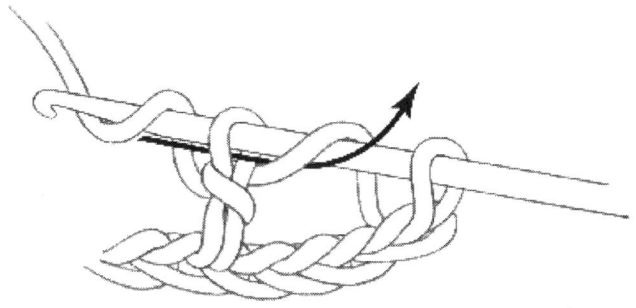

5. Yarn over. Draw the yarn through two loops. Yarn over. Draw the yarn through two loops. Yarn over, and draw the yarn through two loops. Continue.

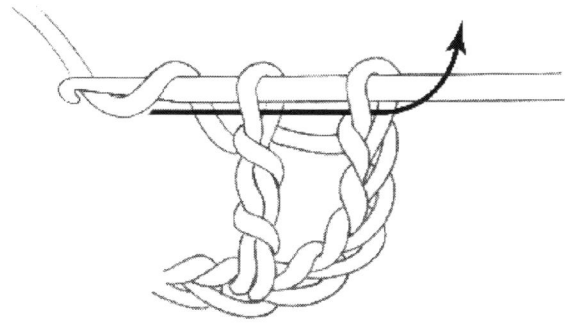

**Fastening Off**

6. When the crochet is as long as you would like, finish the last row and cut the yarn, leaving 6 inches.

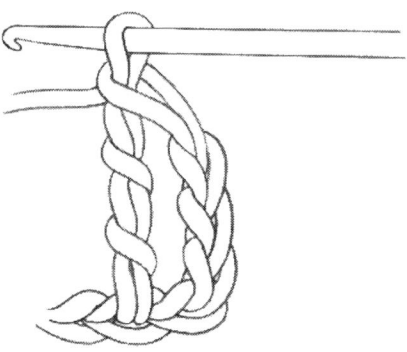

7. Draw the hook straight up through the stitch bringing the 6-inch thread completely through. Pull it tightly to close.

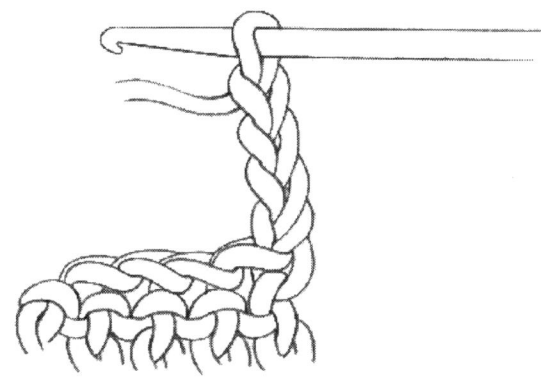

# Tunisian Simple Stitch

1. Start with one slip knot and 12 chains. Do not turn the fabric.

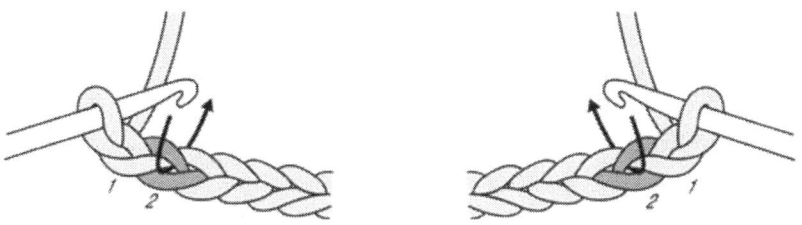

## Forward Pass Stitch

2. First row. You will keep all the chains on the hook. Hook the needle into the second chain. Yarn over.

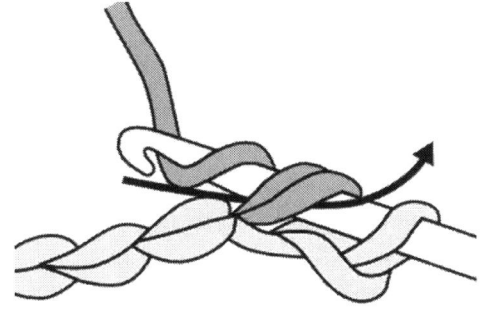

3. Pull the yarn through the second chain. Continue to yarn over and pull through. Keep all the loops on the crochet hook. At the end of the row, do not turn.

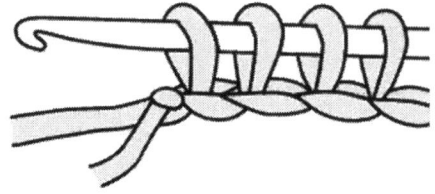

## Return Pass

4. Do not turn the fabric. Yarn over. Pull through the first loop. For the rest of the row, yarn over and pull through two loops at a time, until only one loop is left on your hook.

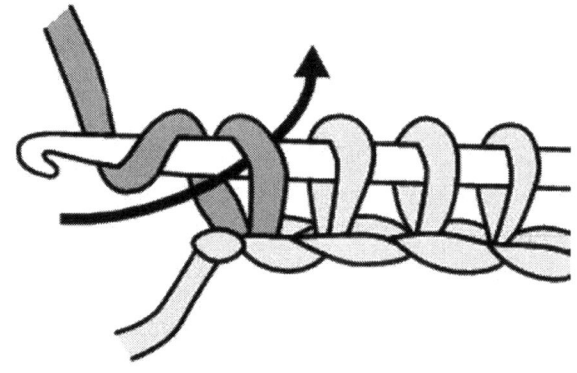

## Second Row

5. Now the first foundation row is completed. You will continue the same forward pass stitch, but you will insert the crochet hook in the vertical bar at the front

of the fabric. Skip the first vertical bar. Insert the crochet hook in the second vertical bar.

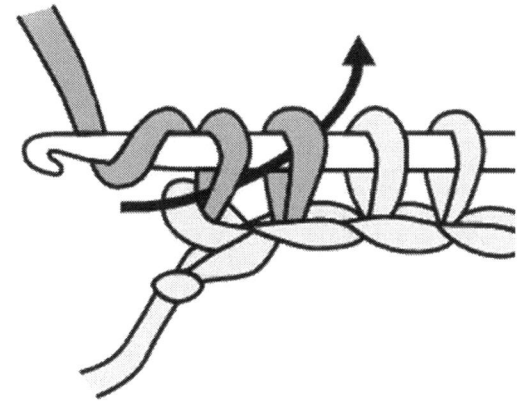

6. Yarn over. Pull the yarn through the second vertical bar. Continue to yarn over and pull through. Keep all the loops on the crochet hook as in row 1. At the end of the row, do not turn, do the return pass stitch.

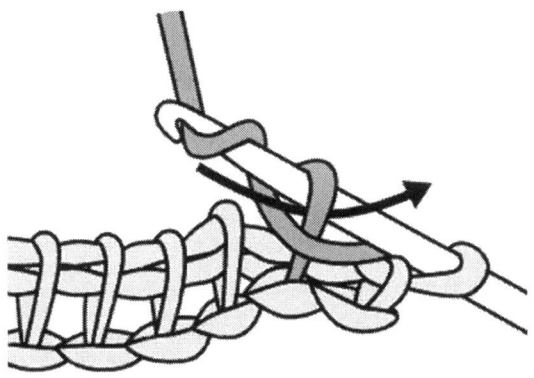

**Fastening Off**

7. When the crochet is as long as you would like it, finish the last row and cut the yarn, leaving 6 inches.

Draw the hook straight up through the stitch bringing the 6-inch tail completely through. Pull it tightly to close.

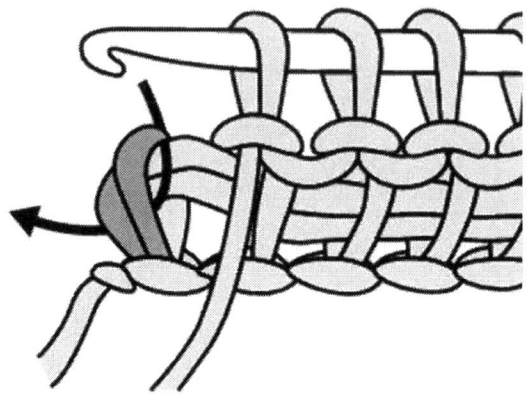

# 1. Soap Saver Bag

## Materials

- Crochet hook 5.5mm

- Crochet hook 5.0mm

- Cotton yarn (for bag)

- Cotton yarn (drawstring)

- Yarn needle

## Gauge

- 1 Inch = 3 rows and 4 stitches

## Directions

1. With the 5.5mm hook crochet 11 chains. **Row 1:** Single crochet in the 2nd chain from hook, and in each chain across. You will now have 10 single crochets. Turn.

2. **Row 2:** Chain 1, single crochet in each stitch across. You will have 10 single crochets. Turn.

3. **Row 3:** (you will now start to make a round bag shape): Chain 1 and make 2 single crochets in the first stitch. In each stitch, single crochet until the last stitch of the row and make a 2 single crochet in the last stitch of the row. Work 3 single crochet down the side of the 3 rows. Starting in the bottom loops of the original chain; make 2 single crochet in first chain. Single crochet in each chain until you come to the last chain; then make 2 single crochet in the last chain. Work 3 single crochet up the side of the rows and join in the first single chain. Do not turn as you will now have the round shape. In total, there will be 30 stitches.

4. **Row 4:** Make 4 chains (double chain with a single chain) and skip the next stitch *double crochet into the next stitch, chain 1 and skip the next stitch** Repeat the instructions from * to ** in a circular shape. Join together at the top of turning chain. You should have 15 double crochet stitches.

5. **Round 5:** Make 4 chains (double chain with a single chain), *double chain in chain 1 and create a space with 1 chain** Repeat from * to ** around. Join the round at the top of the turning chain. There will be 15 double crochet stitches.

6. **Rounds 6-9:** continue with the same pattern as in round 5.

7. **Round 10:** Make 1 chain, half double crochet in each chain leaving 1 space and double crochet around. Cut the yarn off leaving a tail and join with an invisible join. (Thread the tail through the yarn needle and insert the needle under the last stitch and pull through. Place the needle through the chain of the next stitch and pull through. Continue until all of the tail is inserted.

8. **Drawstring:** With the 5.0 hook, make a tight chain of 70 chains. Pull the yarn through the last chain leaving a tail. Thread the tail through the yarn needle and start to weave the drawstring the upper half double crochets made in round 10. Knot the two ends together and trim the lose pieces of yarn. Fill the bag with the last bits of soap from the bar and pull the drawstring together.

# 2. Jelly Jar Covers

## Materials

- Crochet hook 3.75mm

- Fine yarn

- Jelly jar with a 3" lid

- Ribbon 1 meter

- Yarn needle

## Gauge

- 3 Inches = 3 rounds

## Directions

1. Crochet 3 chains and make a slip stitch in the first chain to form a ring. **Round 1**: Chain 3 (this will count as the first double crochet right through the pattern), make 11 double crochet into the ring. Join

with a slip stitch into the third chain of the initial 3 chains made. In total, you will have 12 double crochet.

2. **Round 2**: Chain 3, double crochet into same double crochet in round 1. Make 2 double crochet into each double crochet from round 1. Join with a slip stitch into the third chain of the initial 3 chains made. In total, you will have 24 double crochet.

3. **Round 3:** Chain 3, double crochet into the same double crochet in round 2 and double crochet into the next double crochet. *2 double crochet in the next double crochet, double crochet in next dc* Repeat from * 10 more times. Join with a slip stitch in third chain of the beginning of the 3 chains. You will now have a total of 36 double crochet.

4. **Round 4:** Chain 1 (this will count as single crochet), working only in the back-loop stitch, single chain around. Make a slip stitch in the beginning of the first chain and join. You should have made 36 single chains.

5. **Rounds 5 - 7:** Chain 1, *skip the next single crochet and make 2 single crochet in next single crochet* Repeat from * all the way round. To join make a slip stitch into the first single crochet.

6. **Round 8:** (Eyelet round where the ribbon will be threaded through): Chain 3, *skip 2 single crochet and single crochet into the next single crochet, chain

2* Repeat from * all the way round. Join with a slip stitch in first chain of the beginning of the 3 chains.

7. **Round 9:** Slip stitch in the first chain - leave 2 spaces, *single crochet, double crochet, treble crochet, double crochet, single crochet* in every 2nd space. Repeat * all the way around and join with a slip stitch in the first single crochet. Fasten off and cut the yarn.

8. **Finishing:** Weave in the lose yarn ends with a yarn needle. Thread the ribbon through round 8 (the eyelet round) and tie in a bow. Place the cover over the jelly jar.

# 3. Valentine's Day Red Crochet Hearts

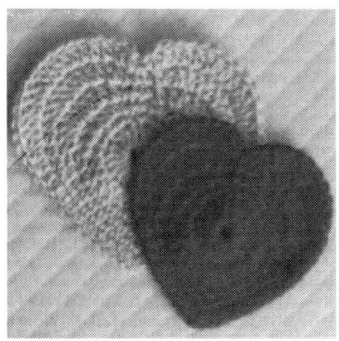

## Materials

- Yarn

- Crochet hook 3.5mm

- Yarn needle

## Gauge

- 1 Inch = 2 ½ rows

## Directions

1. Chain 5 and slip stitch into the first chain to make the ring. **Round 1:** Chain 2 and make 19 double crochets into the ring. Join together with a slip stitch into the top of 1st double crochet.

2. **Round 2:** Chain 1, and then 2 single crochets into the next 2 stitches; make 1 half double crochet into

the next 3 stitches; make 1 double crochet into next 4 stitches; make 3 double crochets into next stitch (this creates the bottom tip of heart); 1 double crochet into the next 4 stitches; 1 half double crochet into the next 3 stitches; 2 single crochets into next 2 stitches. To join, make a slip stitch into the 1st single crochet. You will now have a total of 25 stitches.

3. **Round 3:** Chain 1 and make 1 single crochet into the same stitch; make 2 half double crochets in next stitch; 1 double crochet into the next 4 stitches; 1 half double crochet into the next 2 stitches; 1 single crochet into the next 4 stitches; 3 single crochets into the next stitch (this should be in the middle of the single crochet of the 3-single crochet tip of the row below); 1 single crochet in next 4 stitches; 1 half double crochet into the next 2 stitches; 1 double crochet into next 4 stitches; 2 half double crochets into the next stitch; 1 single crochet in next stitch. To join, make a slip stitch to the 1st single crochet. You will now have a total of 29 stitches.

4. **Round 4:** Chain 1and make 1 single crochet into same stitch; make 1 double crochet into the next stitch; 2 double crochets into the next 4 stitches; 1 single crochet into the next 8 stitches; 3 single crochets into the next stitch (you should now be at the tip of the heart); 1 single crochet into the next 8 stitches; 2 double crochets into the next 4 stitches; 1 double crochet into the next stitch; 1 single crochet into the next stitch. To join, make a slip stitch to 1st

single crochet. You will now have a total of 39 stitches.

5. **Round 5:** Chain 1 and make 1 single crochet into the same stitch; make 2 double crochets into the next 3 stitches, 1 double crochet into the next stitch; 2 double crochets into the next stitch; 1 double crochet into the next stitch; 1 half double crochet into next 4 stitches; 2 single crochets into the next stitch; 1 single crochet into the next 7 stitches; 3 single crochets into the next stitch (you should now be at the tip of the heart); 1 single crochet into the next 7 stitches; 2 single crochets into the next stitch; 1 half double crochet into the next 4 stitches; 1 double crochet into the next stitch; 2 double crochets into the next stitch; 1 double crochet in next stitch; 2 double crochets into the next 3 stitches; 1 single crochet into the next stitch. To join, make a slip stitch to 1st single crochet. You will end with a total of 51 stitches. Fasten off the yarn with a knot and thread the excess yarn through the heart.

# 4. Baby Bath Wash Cloths

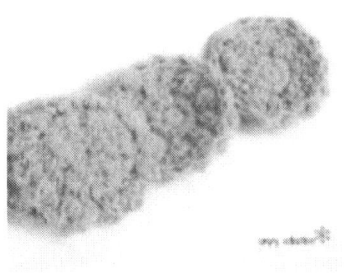

## Materials

- Crochet hook 5.5mm

- Cotton yarn

- Yarn needle

## Directions

1. **Round 1:** Chain 2 and then 6 single crochet in the 2nd chain. Join with a slip stitch; chain 1(do not turn when you make the chain).

2. **Round 2:** 2 single crochet into each stitch. Join with a slip stitch; chain 1and turn. You will now have 12 stitches.

3. **Round 3:** Treble crochet in same stitch as the turning chain; single crochet and treble crochet into the next stitch. *single crochet, treble crochet and single crochet into the next stitch; treble crochet,

single crochet and treble crochet* Repeat the pattern twice from *; single crochet, treble crochet and single crochet in the last stitch. Join with a slip stitch, ch1and turn. You will now have 18 stitches.

4. **Round 4:** Treble crochet into the same stitch as turning chain. Into the next stitch, single crochet, treble crochet, and a single crochet. *treble crochet, single crochet, treble crochet and single crochet in same stitch* Repeat the pattern from * around 5 times; treble crochet and single crochet into the last stitch. Join with a slip stitch. You will now have 24 stitches. Fasten off the yarn and sew in the loose ends.

# 5. Infinity Cowl Scarf

## Materials

- Crochet hook 10.5mm

- Chunky yarn

## Directions

1. Chain 80 and join the chain to the first stitch with a slip stitch. Depending on how long you want the scarf to be, you can add or reduce the number of chains.

2. **Row 1:** Chain 3 and then double crochet in first chain from the hook. Continue with a double crochet in each chain working your way around the circle. Join with slip stitch to the first double crochet.

3. **Row 2:** Chain 4, skip the first double crochet and make a *treble crochet in the following double crochet, chain 1and skip the next double crochet*

Repeat the pattern from * and continue around the circle. At the end, join with a slip stitch.

4. **Row 3:** Chain 4, and make a treble crochet in the space of the first chain of the previous row. *Chain 1, treble crochet in the space of next chain*. Repeat the pattern from *all the way around the circle. Join together with a slip stitch.

5. **Row 4:** Repeat the instruction from row 3.

6. **Row 5:** Chain 3, *double crochet into the next treble crochet, double crochet in the chain 1 space* Repeat the pattern * around the circle. Join the yarn with a slip stitch. Fasten off the yarn and tuck in the ends.

# 6. Easy Crochet Coffee Cozy

## Materials

- Scrap yarn

- Crochet hook 6mm

- Button

- Needle and thread

- Scissors

## Directions

1. Chain 10. **Row 1:** Single chain into the second chain from hook and into each following chain and turn. You should have 9 single crochets.

2. **Row 2:** Chain 1, single crochet into the first single crochet. Continue to single crochet into the one below. Turn. Repeat row 2 until your piece measures about 8 ¾ ". To make sure that this is the right size, measure against your favorite mug. The

piece should cover the mug completely with a slight overlap. If you are a Starbucks fiend, this length will be sufficient.

3. **Buttonhole:** Slip stitch into the first four single crochets; make 6 chains; skip fifth single crochet and slip stitch into the last four single crochets. This loop will be big enough for a 25-28mm button. To accommodate a smaller button, reduce the number of chains when making the loop.

4. **Border:** Make 2 single crochets in the corner stitch, single crochet all along the edge until you reach the next corner. Make 2 single crochets in the corner stitch and then single crochet along short edge. Make 1 single crochet in the bottom corner and continue until you reach the final corner. Single crochet once in the corner and in the first 3 slip stitches; slip stitch in the 4th single crochet; slip stitch in each of the chains where you have the button loop; single stitch in the next slip stitch and then single crochet in the last 3 stitches. Join the yarn and weave in the ends. Wrap your coffee cozy around a mug to check where the button needs to be and sew into place.

# 7. Easy to Crochet Tote Bag

## Materials

- 3 Balls chunky yarn (black – strand A)

- 3 Balls chunky yarn (purple – strand B)

- Crochet hook 8mm

- Metal buckle (4mm)

## Gauge

- 4" = 4 rows of double crochet (2 strands of yarn)

## Directions

1. Front and Back (to be made exactly the same). Using 1 strand each of A and B together, make 32 chains.

2. **Foundation row:** (this will be the wrong side). Make 1 single crochet into the 2nd chain from hook. Make 1 single crochet into each chain until you have

reached the end of the chain. In total, there will be 31 single crochets and turn.

3. **Row 1:** Chain 3 (this will count as a double crochet). Make 1 double crochet into each single crochet to the end of the row. Turn.

4. **Row 2:** Chain 1. Make 1 single crochet into each double crochet until the end of the row. Turn. Repeat these 2 rows until work measures 14 inches. End with row 2. Fasten off.

## Flap

1. Using 1 strand each of A and B together, make 9 chains.

2. **Foundation row:** (this will be the wrong side). Make 1 single crochet into the 2nd chain from hook. Make 1 single crochet into each chain until you reach the end of chain. In total, there will be 8 single crochets and turn.

3. **Row 1:** Chain 3 (this will count as a double crochet). Make 1 double crochet into each single crochet until the end of the row. Turn.

4. **Row 2:** Chain 1. Make 1 single crochet into each double crochet until the end of the row. Turn.

5. **Repeat row 1 and 2, 5 more times.**

6. **Row 13:** (this will be the right side). Chain1. Draw up a loop in each of next 2 single crochets. With the yarn over the hook, draw through all 3 loops onto the hook – this will make a single crochet 2together. Make 1 single crochet into each of next 4 single crochets. Single crochet 2together over last 2 single crochets. 6 stitches and turn.

7. **Row 14:** Chain 1. Single crochet 2 together over the first 2 stitches and make 1 single crochet into each of next 2 single crochets. Over the next 2 stitches, single crochet 2together. 4 stitches and turn.

8. **Row 15:** Chain 1. Single crochet 2 together over first 2 stitches; then over the next 2 stitches, single crochet 2 together. 2 stitches and fasten off the yarn.

**Handles (you will need to make 2 handles)**

1. Using 1 strand each of A and B together, chain 69. **Row 1:** (this will be the right side). Chain 1. Make 1 single crochet into each chain until the end of the chain and turn.

2. **Row 2:** Chain 1. Make 1 single crochet into each single crochet until the end of the row. Turn. Repeat row 1 and 2 until the length measures 4 inches. Fasten off.

**Finishing**

1. Place together the wrong side of the front and back. Sew together the side and bottom seams. On the

upper edge, place markers 3 inches in from side seams.

2. Fold lengthwise each handle in half. Sew together the foundation and last row. Using the markers as a guide, sew the handles to the upper edges of the bag.

3. Place the foundation row of the flap on the back of the bag and center. Move approximately 2 inches below the upper edge. Sew into position. Fold the flap over the upper edge of the bag. On the front of the bag, mark the position of the buckle. Sew the buckle to the front of the bag.

# 8. Simple Slouch Beanie

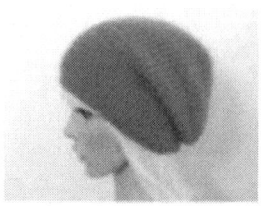

## Materials

- Medium weight yarn

- Crochet hook 5 mm

- Crochet hook 4 mm

- Tapestry needle

## Gauge

- 14 Double crochets x 9 rows = 4 inches

## Directions

1. Start off the hat by making a magic loop. **Row 1:** Chain 2 (this will count as the first double crochet) and then make 11 double crochets into the ring. Join to the top of chain 2 and pull loop tight (you will have 12 stitches).

2. **Row 2:** Chain 2 (this will count as the first double crochet), double crochet into the same stitch, *2

double crochets into the next stitch* all the way round and join (you will now have 24 stitches).

3. **Row 3:** Chain 2 (this will count as the first double crochet), double crochet into the next stitch, 2 double crochets in next stitch, *double crochet into the next 2 stitches, 2 double crochets into the next stitch*. Repeat from * all the way round and join (you will now have 32 stitches).

4. **Row 4:** Chain 2 (this will count as the first double crochet), 2 double crochets into the next stitch, *double crochet into the next 3 stitches, 2 double crochets into the next stitch*. Repeat from * all the way round and join. (You will now have 40 stitches).

5. **Row 5:** Chain 2 (this will count as the first double crochet), 2 double crochets into the next stitch, *double crochet into the next 4 stitches, 2 double crochets into the next stitch*. Repeat from * all the way round and join. (You will now have 48 stitches). **Row 6:** Chain 2 (this will count as the first double crochet), 2 double crochets into the next stitch, *double crochet into the next 5 stitches, 2 double crochets into the next stitch*. Repeat from * all the way round and join. (You will now have 56 stitches).

6. **Row 7:** Chain 2 (this will count as the first double crochet), 2 double crochets into the next stitch, *double crochet into the next 6 stitches, 2 double crochets into the next stitch*. Repeat from * all the

way round and join. (You will now have 64 stitches).

7. **Row 8:** Chain 2 (this will count as the first double crochet), 2 double crochets into the next stitch, *double crochet into the next 7 stitches, 2 double crochets into the next stitch*. Repeat from * all the way round and join. (You will now have 72 stitches).

8. **Row 9:** Chain 2, *double crochet in each stitch*. Repeat from * all the way round and join. **Rows 10-28:** Repeat the pattern in Row 9 and join. **Note:** Depending on how long you would like the slouch to be or the tension gauge, you will be able to add on or reduce the number of rows crochet.

9. **Row 29:** Switch to the smaller hook. Chain 1, *in back loop only, single crochet in each stitch. * Repeat from * all the way round and join. **Rows 30-34:** Repeat the pattern in Row 29. Fasten off the yarn and weave in the loose ends.

# 9. Crochet Pot Holder

## Materials

- Worsted weight yarn (plain or multi-colored)

- Crochet hook 6 mm

- Tapestry needle

## Directions

1. Crochet 19 chains.

2. **Row 1:** Single crochet into the 2$^{nd}$ chain from the hook. *Single crochet into the next chain* Repeat from * all the way across. Chain 1and turn. (You will have 18 stitches).

3. **Row 2:** *Single crochet into the next stitch*. Repeat from * all the way across. Chain 1and turn. (You will have 18 stitches). Repeat Row 2 another 20 times, or until you have reached a required length.

4. **DO NOT FASTEN OFF.**

5. Chain 5 and make a slip stitch in the beginning stitch to form a loop. Fasten off and weave in the loose ends.

# 10. Crochet Boot Cuffs

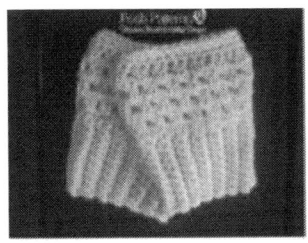

## Materials

- Worsted weight yarn

- Crochet hook 2.25 mm

- Tapestry needle

## Directions

1. Crochet 12 chains. **Row 1:** Single crochet into the 2nd chain from hook. *Single crochet into the next chain*. Repeat the pattern from * all the way across. Chain 1 and turn. (You will have 11 stitches).

2. **Row 2-30:** (work only in the back loop) *Single crochet into the next stitch*. Repeat from * all the way across. Chain 1 and turn. (You will have 11 stitches).

3. With the short sides together, fold in half. Close the ends together with slip stitches. **NOTE:** From this point onwards, you will start to work in rounds.

4. **Round 31:** Chain 1 and turn piece right side out so that the seam is on the inside. Work 30 single crochet stitches around the edge of cuff. Join to the first stitch. (You will have 30 stitches).

5. **Round 32-35:** Chain 2. Make 2 double crochets into the same stitch, skip 1 stitch. *2 double crochet into the next stitch, skip 1 stitch*. Repeat the pattern from * all the way round and join. Slip stitch into the next stitch and slip stitch into the next space. (You will have 15 double crochet groups).

6. **Round 36-37:** Chain 1and single crochet into the same stitch. *Single crochet into the next stitch*. Repeat pattern from * all the way round and join. Fasten off the yarn and weave in loose ends.

# 11. Light and Simple Shawl

## Materials

- Light weight yarn 12.25 oz.

- Crochet hook 4.25 mm

- Tapestry needle

## Directions

1. Crochet 91 chains. **Row 1:** Make a single crochet in the second chain from the hook. *chain 3, skip 2 chains, single crochet in the next chain*. Repeat this pattern until you have reached the last 2 chains. Chain 3; skip a chain and single crochet into the last chain. (You will now have 30 chains with 3 spaces).

2. **Row 2:** Chain 4. (This will count as a double crochet and 1 chain). Turn your work around, *single crochet into chain 3 from the previous row, chain 1, double crochet in the very next single crochet from the row below, and chain 1 again*. Repeat the pattern from * a further 39 times. Single

crochet in the last chain 3 spaces from the row below; make 1chain; and double crochet into the last single crochet. (You will now have a total of 31 double crochets in this row).

3. **Row 3:** Chain 1 to start the row and turn. Make a single crochet into the first double crochet. Then *chain 3, skip over the next single crochet, the next chain 1 AND the next single crochet, and make a single crochet into the next double crochet*. Repeat from * across the row and then single crochet into the 3rd chain from the 4th chain from the row below. Repeat rows 2 and 3 until such time as your shawl is to the required length.

# 12. Crochet Holiday Pinecones

## Materials

- Cotton yarn

- Crochet hook 5.5 mm

- Tapestry needle

## Directions

1. Start off the pines by making a magic loop. The pine cones will be made in rounds. **Round 1:** 6 single crochets into the ring and pull closed. **Round 2:** Make 2 single crochet in each single crochet all the way round (You will now have 12 single crochets). **Round 3:** * single crochet into the next single crochet * repeat from * all the way round (You will now have 18 single crochets).

2. **Round 4:** * single crochet into the next two single crochet, increase into the next * repeat pattern * all

the way round (You will now have 24 single crochets). **Round 5:** * single crochet into the next three single crochet, increase into the next * repeat pattern * all the way round (You will now have 30 single crochets).

3. **Round 6 a:** In the front loops only, *slip stitch and chain 3 into one stitch, double crochet into next, slip stitch into the next - 3 stitches* repeat pattern * all the way round, chain 1 (You will now have 10 "petals" plus chain 1). **Round 6 b:** In the back loops of round 5, *single crochet into the next 8, decrease once* repeat pattern * all the way round, join, chain 1 (You will now have 27 single crochets). **Round 7:** Single crochet into each single crochet all the way round (You will have 27 single crochets).

4. **Round 8 a:** In the front loops only, *slip stitch and chain 3 into one stitch, double crochet into the next, slip stitch into the next - 3 stitches* repeat pattern * all the way round, chain 1 (You will now have 9 "petals" plus chain 1). **Round 8 b:** In the back loops of round 7, *single crochet into the next 7, decrease once* repeat the pattern * all the way round, join, chain 1 (You will now have 24 single crochets). **Round 9:** Single crochet into each single crochet all the way round (You will now have 24 single crochets).

5. **Round 10 a:** In the front loops only, *slip stitch and chain 3 in one stitch, double crochet into next, slip stitch into next - 3 stitches* repeat the pattern * all the way round, chain 1 (You will now have 8

"petals" plus chain 1). **Round 10 b:** In the back loops of round 9, *single crochet into the next 6, decrease once* repeat the pattern * all the way round, join, chain 1 (You will now have 21 single crochets). **Round 11:** Single crochet in each single crochet all the way round (You will now have 21 single crochets).

6. **Round 12 a:** In the front loops only, *slip stitch and chain 3 in one stitch, double crochet into the next, slip stitch into the next - 3 stitches* repeat the pattern * all the way round, chain 1 (You will now have 7 "petals" plus chain 1). **Round 12 b:** In the back loops of round 11, *single crochet into the next 5, decrease once* repeat the pattern * all the way round, join, chain 1 (You will now have 18 single crochets). **Round 13:** Single crochet into each single crochet all the way round (You will now have 18 single crochet).

7. **Round 14 a:** In the front loops only, *slip stitch and chain 3 in one stitch, double crochet into the next, slip stitch into the next - 3 stitches* repeat pattern * all the way round, chain 1 (You will now have 6 "petals" plus chain 1). **Round 14 b:** In the back loops of round 13, *single crochet into the next 4, decrease once* repeat the pattern * all the round, join, chain 1 (You will now have 15 single crochets). **Round 15:** Single crochet into each single crochet all the way round (You will now have 15 single crochets).

8. **Round 16 a:** In the front loops only, *slip stitch and chain 3 in one stitch, double crochet into the next, slip stitch into the next - 3 stitches* repeat pattern * all the way round, chain 1 (You will now have 5 "petals" plus chain 1). **Round 16 b:** In the back loops of round 15, *single crochet into the next 3, decrease once* repeat the pattern * all the way round, join, chain 1 (You will now have 12 single crochets). **Round 17:** Single crochet into each single crochet all the way round (You will now have 12 single crochets).

9. **Round 18 a:** In the front loops only, *slip stitch and chain 3 in one stitch, double crochet into the next, slip stitch into the next - 3 stitches* repeat pattern * all the way round, chain 1 (You will now have 4 "petals" plus chain 1). **Round 18 b:** In the back loops of round 17, *single crochet into the next 2, decrease once* repeat the pattern * all the way round, join, chain 1 (You will now have 9 single crochets). **Round 19:** Single crochet into each single crochet all the way round (You will now have 9 single crochets). **Round 20:** In the front loops only, *slip stitch and chain 3 into one stitch, double crochet into the next, slip stitch into the next - 3 stitches* repeat the pattern * all the way round (You will now have 3 "petals"). Fasten off the yarn and thread through the loose ends.

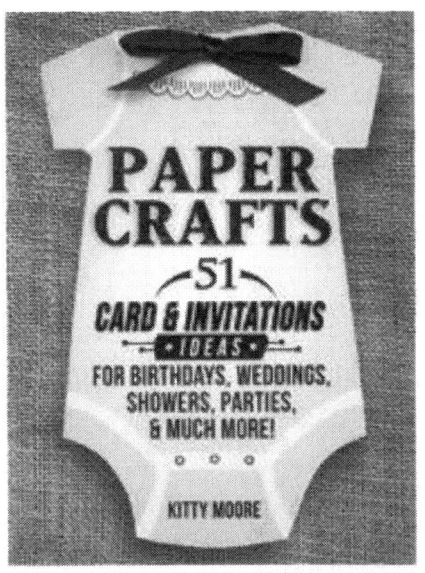

## Check out Kitty's books at:

## ArtsCraftsAndMore.com/go/books

# 13. Warm and Soft Baby Blanket

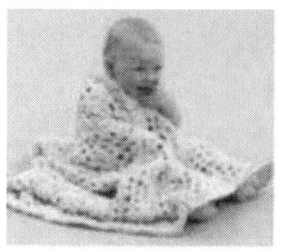

## Materials

- 3 Balls Lion Brand Velvetspun yarn or similar (A)

- 3 Balls Lion Brand Velvetspun yarn or similar (B)

- 1 Ball Lion Brand Babysoft yarn or similar (C)

- 1 Ball Lion Brand Babysoft yarn or similar (D)

- Crochet hook 6.5 mm

- Tapestry needle

## Gauge

- 7 ½ inches x 7 ½ inches equals 1 square (change size of crochet hook to accommodate if necessary)

## Directions

**Square 1 – you will need to make 13 squares**

1. Starting with yarn A; chain 3 and join with a slip stitch to form a ring. **Round 1:** (This will be the right side) Chain 3 and make 2 double crochets into the ring, chain 2, *3 double crochet, chain 2* repeat the pattern * 3 times into the ring. Join with a slip stitch in the top of the beginning of the chain 4 corner and chain 2 spaces. Fasten off yarn A.

2. **Round 2:** With the right side facing, join 1 strand each of yarn C and yarn D in the corner of the chain 2 space and work holding the 2 yarns together. Chain 3, **2 double crochet, chain 3, 3 double crochet* in same chain 2 space, chain 1, *3 double crochet, chain 3, 3 double crochet, chain 1**. Repeat pattern from ** to ** in each chain 2 space all the way round. Join with slip stitch in the top of the beginning of chain 4 corner chain 3 spaces.

3. **Round 3:** Make a slip stitch to first chain 3 space, chain 3, (2 double crochet, chain 3, 3 double crochet) in same chain 3 space, chain 1, (3 double crochet, chain 1) into the next chain 1 space, *3 double crochet, chain 3, 3 double crochet, chain 1 into the next chain 3 space; 3 double crochet, chain 1 into the next chain 1 space* Repeat the pattern from * all the way round. Join with a slip stitch in the top of the beginning chain 4 corner chain 3 spaces; 2 chain 1 space on each side. Fasten off C and D yarn.

4. **Round 4:** With the right side facing, join yarn B in any corner where there is a chain 3 space. Chain 3, 2 double crochet, chain 3, 3 double crochet in the

same chain 3 space, chain 1, *(3 double crochet, chain 1) in each of next 2 chain 1 spaces, 3 double crochet, chain 3, 3 double crochet, chain 1 into the next chain 3 space* Repeat the pattern from * all the way round, ending at *. Join with a slip stitch in top of the beginning of the chain 4 corner chain 3 spaces; 3 chain into the 1 space on either side. Fasten off yarn B.

## Square 2 – you will need to make 12 squares

1. Crochet the same pattern as Square 1, but working in the following color sequence: Use Yarn B for the center ring as well as Round 1.

2. **Rounds 2 and 3:** Using 1 strand each of yarn C and D hold the two yarns together.

3. **Round 4:** Work with yarn A.

## Assembly

1. Joining Row: Holding the wrong sides together of 2 squares facing one another, match stitches across one side. Working through double thickness, join yarn C in any corner stitch, slip stitch into the back loop of each stitch all the way across to next corner.

2. Fasten off yarn C. Join squares together in five strips as follows: Strip A - make 3 strips in the following order: Square 1; Square 2; Square 1; Square 2; Square 1.

3. Strip B - make 2 strips in the following order: Square 2; Square 1; Square 2; Square 1; Square 2.

4. Alternate the two assembled strips and join by working one long joining row across each strip. (Strip A; strip B; strip A; strip B; strip A). Weave in the ends of the yarn.

# 14. Beautiful Baby Booties

## Materials

- Worsted weight yarn (main color)

- Worsted weight yarn (contrasting color / optional)

- Crochet hook 3.75 mm (or appropriate size to fit with gauge)

- Ribbon

- Tapestry needle

## Gauge

- 1" equals 2 double crochet rows and 1" equals 4 double crochet stitches

## Directions

1. **Round 1:** Chain 12. Crochet into the back loop and double crochet into the third chain from the hook

(throughout the patter, this will count as a stitch when you count at the end of a row). Double crochet into the next 8 stitches and then 4 double crochet into the next stitch. (This will allow you to turn and work in the other side of the stitches. In other words, what was the front loop becomes the back loop). Through the back loops, double crochet into the next 8 stitches. Make 2 double crochets into the last stitch. Join with slip stitch. (You will now have 24 stitches)

2. **Round 2:** Chain 2. Double crochet into the bottom of the chain 2 space, 2 double crochet into the next stitch. Double crochet into the next 8 stitches and 2 double crochets into each of the next 4 stitches. Double crochet into the next 8 stitches and 2 double crochets in each of the last 2 stitches. Join with a slip stitch and chain 2. (You will now have 32 stitches)

3. **Round 3:** Double crochet into the back loops of each stitch all the way round. Join and chain 2.

4. **Round 4:** Double crochet into the next 11 stitches. Double crochet 2 together 4 times. Double crochet into the next 12 stitches, join and chain 2. (You will now have 28 stitches)

5. **Round 5:** Double crochet into the next 3 stitches. Double crochet 2 together all the way round until the last 4 stitches. Double crochet into the last 4 stitches, join and chain 2.

6. **Round 6:** Double crochet into each stitch all the way round. Join and chain 2. (You will now have 18 stitches)

7. **Round 7:** Double crochet into the bottom of chain 2 space. * 1 double crochet into the next stitch, 2 double crochet into the next stitch * Repeat the pattern from * all the way round. Double crochet into the last stitch and join. Fasten off the yarn and weave in loose ends.

## Finishing

1. Thread ribbon through round 6 of the bootie and tie in a bow. Alternatively, chain 65 for a tie and leave a 1 ½" to 2" tail. To make a pom-pom, wrap the yarn around a ruler 30 times. Tie in the middle with a piece of yarn and cut the folded edges to make the pom-pom. Thread the tie through round 6 and tie a pom-pom to each end of tie.

## Variations

**Option 1:** Using 2 different colors of yarn, alternate the colors on each round to make stripes.

**Option 2:** Use two colors of yarn, one being the main color (MC) and a contrasting color (CC). Use CC for rounds 1, 2, 7 as well as for tie and pom-poms. Use the MC yarn for all other rounds.

# 15. Gingerbread Man

## Materials

- 4 Ply worsted weight yarn (shades of brown)

- Crochet hook

- Sequins or beads (to be used for the eyes, mouth and buttons)

- Glue

## Directions

### Head

1. **Round 1:** Chain 3, 11 half double crochets in 3rd chain from the hook. Join with a slip stitch in the top of ch-2. (You will now have 12 stitches)

2. **Round 2:** Chain 1, 2 single crochets in each stitch all the way round. Join with slip stitch in first single crochet and fasten off. Leave 6" of yarn for attaching to the body. (You will now have 24 stitches)

## Body and arms

1. **Row 1:** Chain 9, single crochet in 2nd chain from hook, single crochet into each chain all the way across, turn. (You will have 8 stitches)

2. **Rows 2 to 8:** Chain 1, single crochet into each stitch, all the way across and turn. Do not turn or fasten off the yarn at the end of the last row.

3. **Row 9:** For first arm, working at the ends of the rows, chain 1, single crochet into each of the next 3 rows. Leave the remaining rows unworked and turn.

4. **Rows 10 to 11:** Chain 1. Single crochet into each stitch across and turn.

5. **Row 12:** Chain 1, skip first stitch, 3 single crochet into the next stitch, slip stitch into the last stitch and fasten off.

6. **Row 9:** For the second arm, work in the end of rows on the opposite side of the body. Join the brown yarn with a single crochet in row 6, single crochet into each of the last 2 rows, turn. (You will have 3 stitches)

7. **Rows 10 to 12:** Repeat the same pattern as with that of the first arm. Sew the head to the top of the body between the arms.

## Legs

1. **Row 1:** For first leg, with the wrong side of the body facing you, work on the opposite side of row 1. Join with a single crochet into the first stitch, single crochet into each of the next 3 stitches leaving the remaining stitches unworked, turn. (You will now have 4 stitches)

2. **Rows 2 to 5:** Chain 1, single crochet into each stitch across and turn.

3. **Row 6:** Chain 1, skip first stitch, single crochet into the next stitch, 2 single crochets into the next stitch, 3 single crochets into the last stitch, slip stitch into the end of row 5, fasten off.

4. **Row 1:** For second leg, with the right side of the body facing you work on the opposite side of Row 1. Join with a single crochet in the first stitch, single crochet into each of next 3 stitches, turn. (You will now have 4 stitches)

5. **Rows 2 to 6:** Repeat the same pattern as with that of the first leg.

## Finishing

1. Edging for the Gingerbread Man: Using the left-over yarn from the head, join with a single crochet the first row of the arm near the head. Single crochet into each stitch, all the way round. At the end of each row work with a slip stitch as you go round to the next stitch and join with a slip stitch into the first single crochet. Fasten off the yarn.

2. Around the outer edge of the Gingerbread Man, glue a piece of rickrack, or sew a chain stitch in a different color all the way round the edges.

3. Glue two blue beads or sequins 1/8" apart for the eyes over top of round 1 on the head. Glue three red beads or sequins over bottom of round 1 on the head for the mouth. Glue three green beads or sequins to the front of the body as buttons.

# 16. Halloween Pumpkin Towel Ring

## Materials

- Worsted weight yarn (orange and green)

- Crochet hook 3.75 mm

- Yarn needle

- Metal ring (4")

- Green button

- Black beads

- Button

- Hot glue gun or

*   Black thread and needle

## Gauge

*   Rounds 1 to 3 = 2 ½"

## Directions

### Pumpkin

1.  Chain 6 with the orange yarn; join with a slip stitch to form a ring. **Round 1:** Chain 3 (this will count as the first double crochet) and work 11 more double crochets into the ring. Join with a slip stitch to the top of the beginning chain 3. (You will now have 12 double crochets)

2.  **Round 2:** Chain 3 (this will count as the first double crochet), front post double crochet around the same double crochet. *Double crochet into the next double crochet, front post double crochet around the same double crochet*. Repeat the pattern from * another 11 times; join with a slip stitch to the top of the beginning chain 3. (You will now have 24 stitches)

3.  **Round 3:** Chain 3 (this will count as the first double crochet), double crochet into the same stitch, front post double crochet around the next front post double crochet. *2 double crochet into the next double crochet, front post double crochet around the next front post double crochet*. Repeat the pattern from * another 11 times; join with a slip stitch to the

top of the beginning chain 3. (You will now have 36 stitches)

4. **Round 4:** Chain 3 (this will count as the first double crochet, double crochet into the next double crochet, front post double crochet around the next front post double crochet. *Double crochet into each of the next 2 double crochet, front post double crochet around the next front post double crochet*. Repeat the pattern from * another 11 times; join with a slip stitch to the top of the beginning chain 3. (You will now have 36 stitches)

5. **Rounds 5 - 8:** Repeat round 4.

6. **Round 9:** Chain 2, double crochet into the next double crochet, front post double crochet around the next front post double crochet. *Double crochet decrease over the next 2 double crochet, front post double crochet around the next front post double crochet*. Repeat the pattern from * another 11 times; join with a slip stitch to the top of the beginning chain 3. Fasten off, leaving enough yarn to sew.

**Stem**

1. Using the green yarn, work 1 single crochet around the metal ring and chain 25. **Row 1:** Single crochet into the 2nd chain from hook and in each of the next 23 chains, single crochet around the metal ring and turn.

2. **Row 2:** Skip the single crochet formed around the ring, single crochet into each of the next 20 single crochets, chain 3; skip next 3 single crochet, single crochet into the last single crochet; chain 1 and turn.

3. **Row 3:** Single crochet into the first single crochet, single crochet into each of the next 3 chains; single chain into each of the next 20 single crochet, single crochet around the metal ring. Fasten off yarn.

## Finishing

1. Insert the crochet hook through the ring of the beginning chain 6 of the pumpkin piece, as well as into the buttonhole of the stem piece. Tug the stem piece through the pumpkin piece, so that the pumpkin piece covers the metal ring.

2. Above the pumpkin piece attach the button to the base of the stem.

3. Using the left-over yarn from the pumpkin piece, sew together with a running stitch the last row of the back and front of the pumpkin. Make sure that you leave the bottom part of the metal ring open. Gather slightly by pulling the running stitch thread. Close with a knot and weave in the loose ends. Glue or sew the beads onto the pumpkin to form a face.

# Last Chance to Get YOUR Bonus!

**FOR A LIMITED TIME ONLY** – Get my best-selling book "DIY Crafts: The 100 Most Popular Crafts & Projects That Make Your Life Easier " absolutely FREE!

Readers who have downloaded the bonus book as well have seen the greatest changes in their crafting abilities and have expanded their repertoire of crafts – so it is *highly recommended* to get this bonus book today!

# Get your free copy at:

# ArtsCraftsAndMore.com/Bonus

# Final Words

Thank you for downloading this book!

I really hope that you have been inspired to create your own projects and that you will have a lot of fun crafting.

I do hope that you and your family have found lots of ways to fill lazy afternoons or rainy days in a more fun way.

**If you have enjoyed this book and would like to share your positive thoughts, could you please take 30 seconds of your time to go back and give me a review on my Amazon book page!**

**I really appreciate these reviews because I like to know what people have thought about the book.**

Again, thank you and have fun crafting!

# Disclaimer

**No Warranties:** The authors and publishers don't guarantee or warrant the quality, accuracy, completeness, timeliness, appropriateness or suitability of the information in this book, or of any product or services referenced by this site.

The information in this site is provided on an "as is" basis and the authors and publishers make no representations or warranties of any kind with respect to this information. This site may contain inaccuracies, typographical errors, or other errors.

**Liability Disclaimer**: The publishers, authors, and other parties involved in the creation, production, provision of information, or delivery of this site specifically disclaim any responsibility, and shall not be held liable for any damages, claims, injuries, losses, liabilities, costs, or obligations including any direct, indirect, special, incidental, or consequences damages (collectively known as "Damages") whatsoever and howsoever caused, arising out of, or in connection with the use or misuse of the site and the information contained within it, whether such Damages arise in contract, tort, negligence, equity, statute law, or by way of other legal theory.

Manufactured by Amazon.ca
Bolton, ON

16136312R00048